About Skill Builders Alphabet

by Clareen Arnold

Welcome to RBP Books' Skill Builders series. Like our Summer Bridge Activities collection, the Skill Builders series is designed to make learning both fun and rewarding.

Mastering language skills builds confidence and enhances a student's entire educational experience. A fundamental factor in learning to read is a strong phonics foundation, beginning with an awareness of the alphabet, understanding phonemic relationships and the concept of words, and moving onto word recognition.

The Skill Builders Alphabet book uses a variety of fun activities to introduce children to letters and sounds as well as practicing letter recognition, differentiating between upper- and lowercase, and writing.

Learning is more effective when approached with an element of fun and enthusiasm—just as most children approach life. That's why the Skill Builders combine entertaining and academically sound exercises with eye-catching graphics and fun themes—to make reviewing basic skills at school or home fun and effective, for both you and your budding scholars.

Table of Contents

Name _____

Print the uppercase **A**.

Print the lowercase **a**.

Color Al the Alligator eating an apple.

Do the dot-to-dot 1–10.
Color Allison Anteater.
Color the uppercase letter A's brown.
Color the lowercase letter a's red.

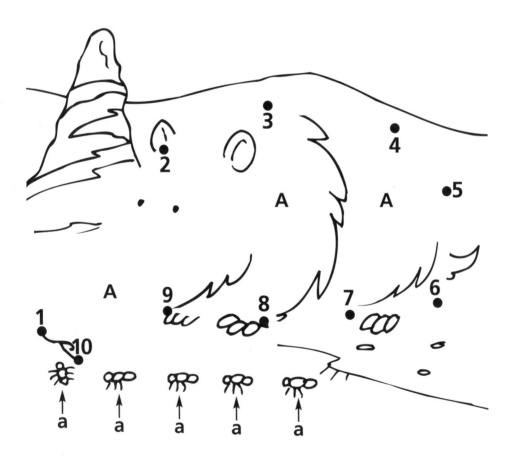

2

Name _____

Aa

Say each picture name.
Listen for the "a" sound.
Draw the pictures on the A, and color them.

Name _____

Bb

Print the uppercase B.

Print the lowercase b.

Color Billy Black Bear bobsledding with his buddies.

Bb

Color the baby birds on the branch.
Color the uppercase letter **B**'s brown.
Color the lowercase letter **b**'s blue.

Name _____

Bb

Say each picture name.
Listen for the "b" sound.
Draw the pictures on the 𝔹, and color them.

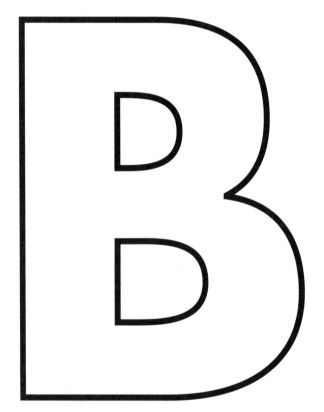

Name _____

Cc

Print the uppercase C.

Print the lowercase C.

Color Cuddles the Cat as she crawls, creeps, and curls up to sleep.

Cc

Do the dot-to-dot 1–10.
Color Carmen Cockroach.
Color the uppercase letter C's red.
Color the lowercase letter C's brown.

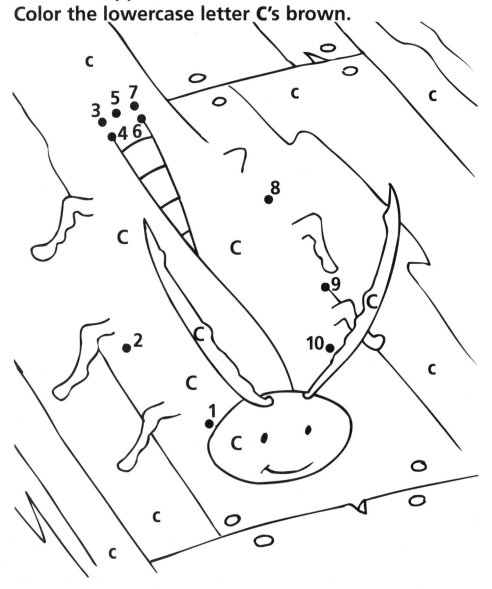

Name _____

Cc

Say each picture name.
Listen for the "c" sound.
Draw the pictures on the ℂ, and color them.

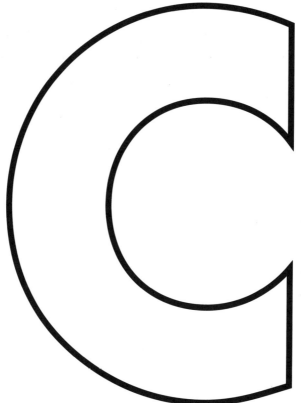

9   Alphabet—RBP3241

Name _____

Dd

Print the uppercase D.

Print the lowercase d.

Color Don the Dog digging in the dirt for bones.

Name _____

Dd

Color Danny the Dinosaur.
Color the uppercase letter D's green.
Color the lowercase letter d's orange.

Name _____

Dd

Say each picture name.
Listen for the "d" sound.
Draw the pictures on the D, and color them.

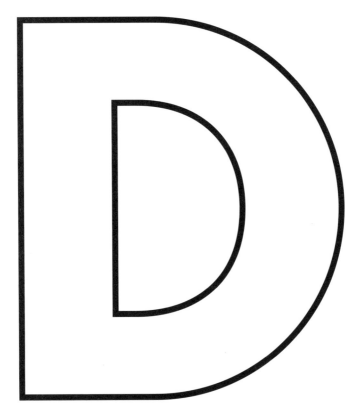

Name _____

Ee

Print the uppercase E.

Print the lowercase e.

Color Eric the Elephant with his extra long nose.

Name _____

Ee

Color Edward the Eagle.
Color the uppercase letter E's brown.
Color the lowercase letter e's orange.

Name _____

Ee

Say each picture name.
Listen for the "e" sound.
Draw the pictures on the E, and color them.

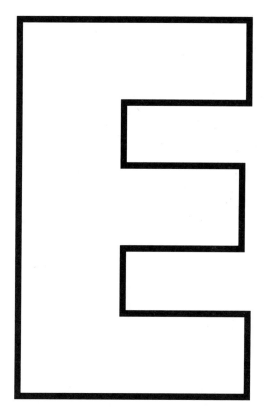

Name _____

F f

Print the uppercase F.

Print the lowercase f.

Color Frank the Frog, who is fit to swim.

Name _____

F f

Do the dot-to-dot 1–10.
Color Fancy Flamingo.
Color the uppercase letter **F**'s orange.
Color the lowercase letter **f**'s pink.

F f

Say each picture name.
Listen for the "f" sound.
Draw the pictures on the F, and color them.

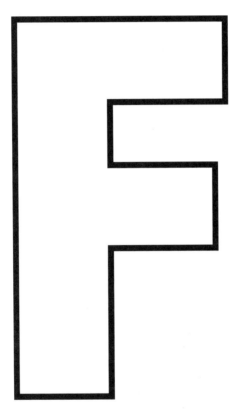

Name _____

Gg

Print the uppercase G.

Print the lowercase g.

Color Gregory the Giraffe gobbling on the grass.

Gg

Do the dot-to-dot 1–10.
Color Gloria Groundhog.
Color the uppercase letter G's brown.
Color the lowercase letter g's green.

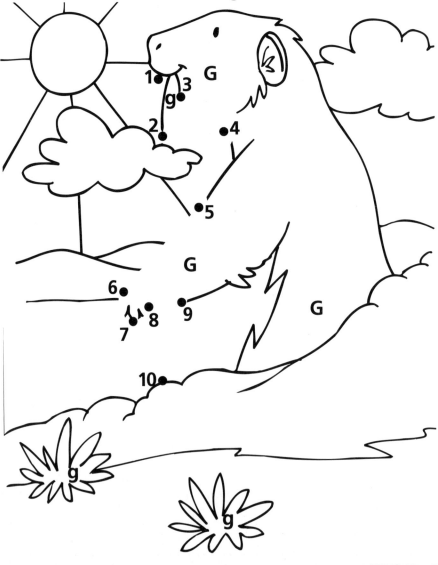

Name _____

Gg

Say each picture name.
Listen for the "g" sound.
Draw the pictures on the G, and color them.

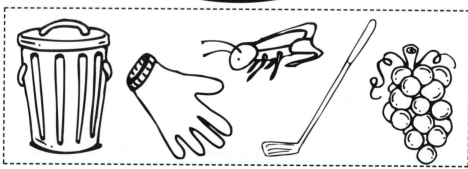

Name _____

Print the uppercase H.

Print the lowercase h.

Color Harry Hippo with his happy family.

Name _____

Hh

Do the dot-to-dot 1–10.
Color Hanna the Horse.
Color the uppercase letter H's gold.
Color the lowercase letter h's brown.

Say each picture name.
Listen for the "h" sound.
Draw the pictures on the H, and color them.

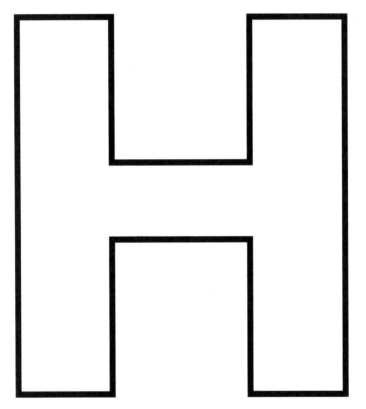

I i

Print the uppercase I.

Print the lowercase i.

Color Icky the Inchworm inching around the leaf.

Name _____

I i

Do the dot-to-dot 1–10.
Color Ike Iguana.
Color the uppercase letter I's green.
Color the lowercase letter i's purple.

Name _____

I i

Say each picture name.
Listen for the "i" sound.
Draw the pictures on the I, and color them.

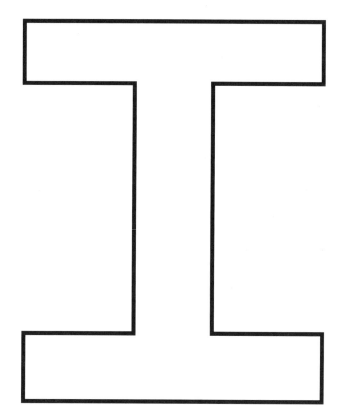

Name _____

J j

Print the uppercase J.

Print the lowercase j.

Color Jimmy the Jackrabbit jumping and jogging.

Jj

Do the dot-to-dot 1–10.
Color Jennifer the Jaguar.
Color the uppercase letter J's yellow.
Color the lowercase letter j's brown.

Jj

Say each picture name.
Listen for the "j" sound.
Draw the pictures on the J, and color them.

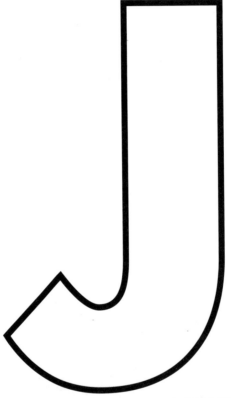

Kk

Print the uppercase K.

Print the lowercase k.

Color Kenny the Kangaroo kissing.

Kk

Color Karen Koala.
Color the uppercase letter K's gray.
Color the lowercase letter k's brown.

Kk

Say each picture name.
Listen for the "k" sound.
Draw the pictures on the K, and color them.

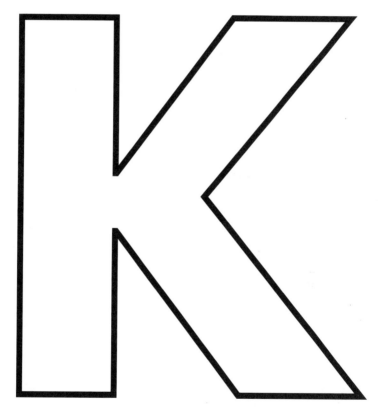

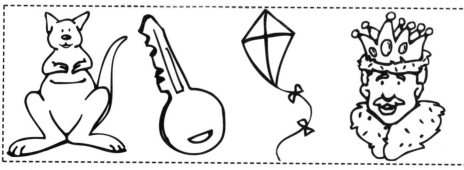

Name _____

L l

Print the uppercase L.

-1 |‾‾‾‾‾‾‾‾‾‾‾‾‾‾‾‾‾‾‾‾‾‾‾‾‾‾‾‾‾‾‾‾‾‾‾‾‾‾
   |- - - - - - - - - - - - - - - - - - -
↓ |2→ _____

Print the lowercase l.

-1 |‾‾‾‾‾‾‾‾‾‾‾‾‾‾‾‾‾‾‾‾‾‾‾‾‾‾‾‾‾‾‾‾‾‾‾‾‾‾
   |- - - - - - - - - - - - - - - - - - -
↓ |_____

Color Leo the Lion lying down, drinking lemonade.

Name _____

L l

Do the dot-to-dot 1–10.
Color Larry the Lizard.
Color the uppercase letter L's green.
Color the lowercase letter l's orange.

L l

Say each picture name.
Listen for the "l" sound.
Draw the pictures on the L, and color them.

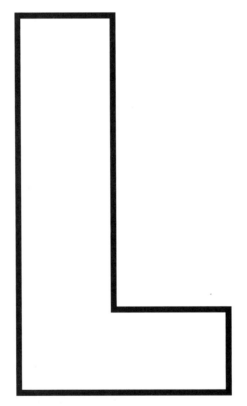

Name _____

Print the uppercase M.

Print the lowercase m.

Color Molly Monkey making music in a tree.

Mm

Color Mitch and Mike Mouse.
Color the uppercase letter **M**'s gray.
Color the lowercase letter **m**'s pink.

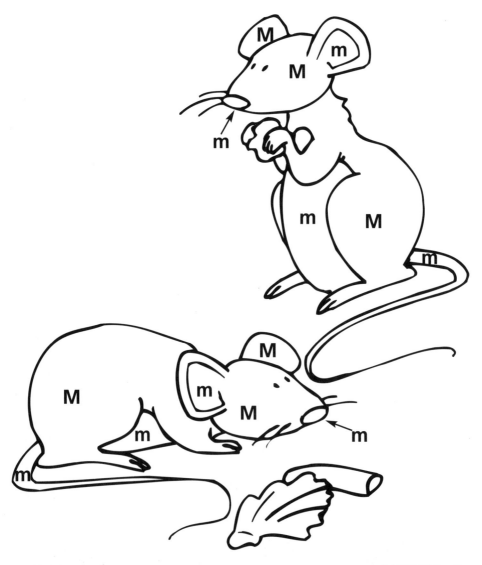

Name _____

Mm

Say each picture name.
Listen for the "m" sound.
Draw the pictures on the M, and color them.

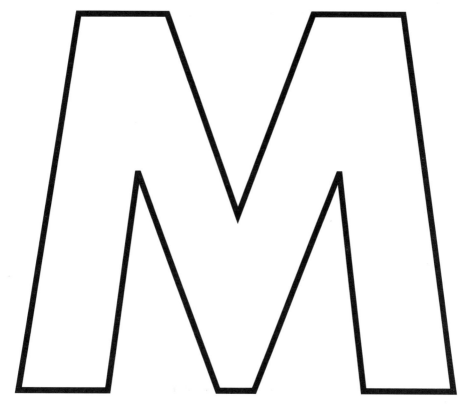

Name _____

Print the uppercase **N**.

Print the lowercase **n**.

Color Nelly Nightingale's nine eggs in her nest.

Nn

Do the dot-to-dot 1–10.
Color Nelly Nightingale.
Color the uppercase letter N's light brown.
Color the lowercase letter n's green.

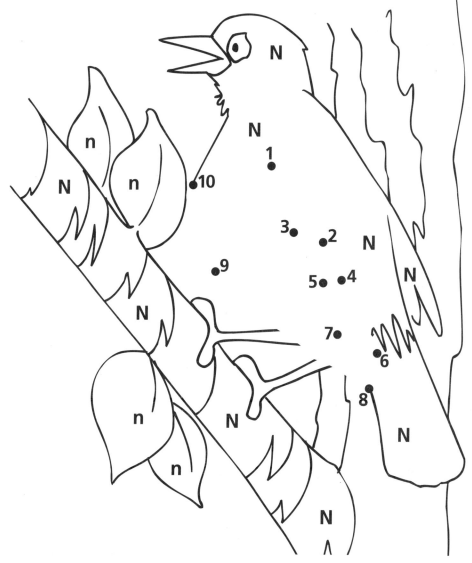

Name _____

Nn

Say each picture name.
Listen for the "n" sound.
Draw the pictures on the N, and color them.

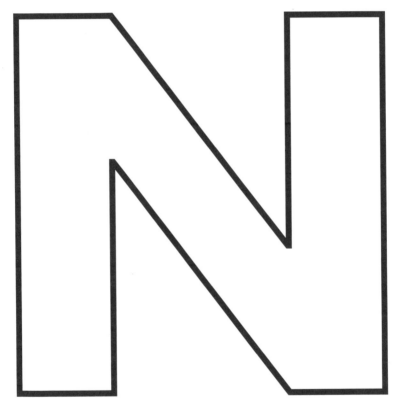

Name _____

Print the uppercase O.

Print the lowercase O.

Color Olive Octopus with her eight arms.

Oo

Color Opal Otter and her offspring.
Color the uppercase letter **O**'s blue.
Color the lowercase letter **O**'s brown.

Name _____

Oo

Say each picture name.
Listen for the "o" sound.
Draw the pictures on the Ⓞ, and color them.

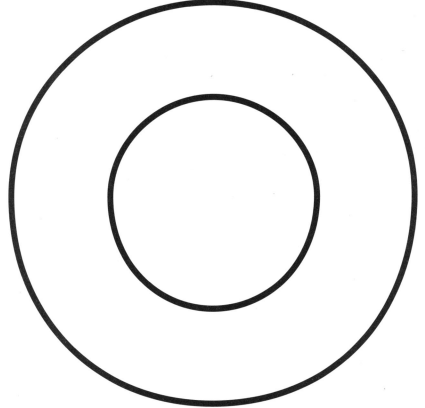

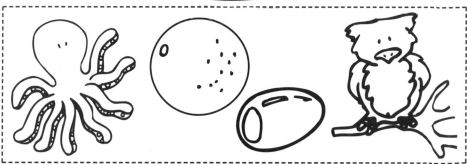

Name _____

Pp

Print the uppercase P.

Print the lowercase p.

Color Penny the Pig in her pretty wig.

Name _____

Pp

Do the dot-to-dot 1–10.
Color Pudgy Parrot.
Color the uppercase letter P's red.
Color the lowercase letter p's orange.

Name _____

Pp

Say each picture name.
Listen for the "p" sound.
Draw the pictures on the ℙ, and color them.

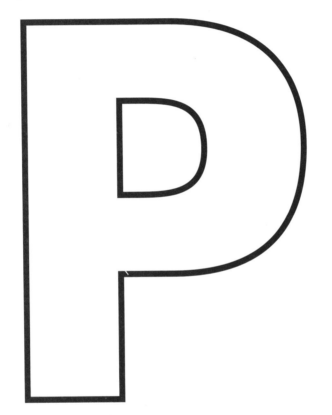

Name _____

Qq

Print the uppercase Q.

Print the lowercase q.

Color Quilla Quail. She is quiet on her quilt.

Name _____

Qq

Do the dot-to-dot 1–10.
Color Queenie Quokka.
Color the uppercase letter Q's brown.
Color the lowercase letter q's green.

Name _____

Qq

Say each picture name.
Listen for the "q" sound.
Draw the pictures on the Q, and color them.

Name _____

R r

Print the uppercase R.

Print the lowercase r.

Color Roxy Raccoon relaxing by the river.

Name _____

Rr

Do the dot-to-dot 1–10.
Color Robert Rooster.
Color the uppercase letter R's red.
Color the lowercase letter r's orange.

53

R r

Say each picture name.
Listen for the "r" sound.
Draw the pictures on the R, and color them.

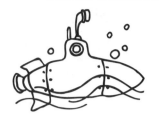

S s

Print the uppercase S.

Print the lowercase s.

Color Sid Spider spiraling down from the ceiling.

S s

Do the dot-to-dot 1–10.
Color Samantha Snake.
Color the uppercase letter **S**'s yellow.
Color the lowercase letter **S**'s orange.

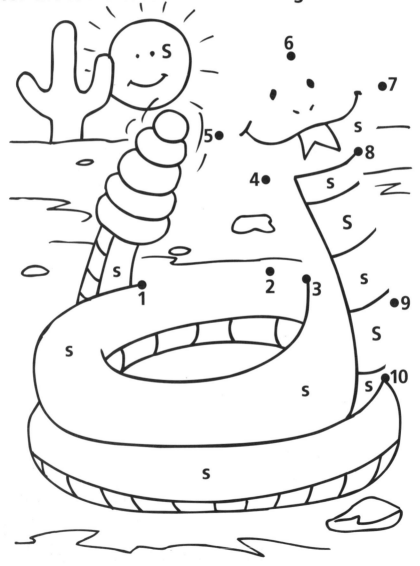

Name _____

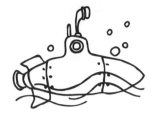

S s

Say each picture name.
Listen for the "s" sound.
Draw the pictures on the S, and color them.

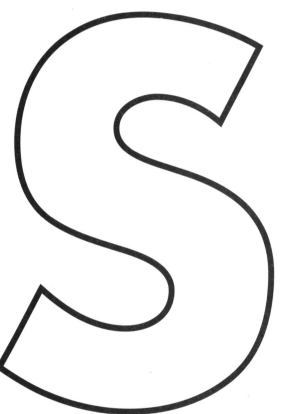

Alphabet—RBP3241

Name _____

T t

Print the uppercase T.

Print the lowercase t.

Color Tommy Turtle tole painting.

T t

Color Tony Tiger.
Color the uppercase letter T's orange.
Color the lowercase letter t's green.

T t

Say each picture name.
Listen for the "t" sound.
Draw the pictures on the T, and color them.

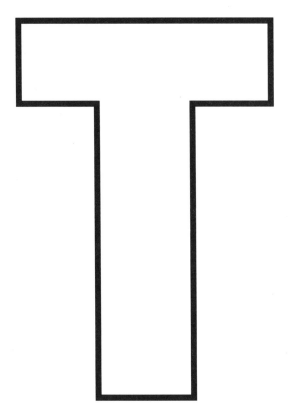

Print the uppercase U.

Print the lowercase u.

Color Usi Unicorn under her umbrella.

Name _____

Uu

Do the dot-to-dot 1–10.
Color Uncle Uakari.
Color the uppercase letter U's brown.
Color the lowercase letter u's red.

Name _____

U u

Say each picture name.
Listen for the "u" sound.
Draw the pictures on the U, and color them.

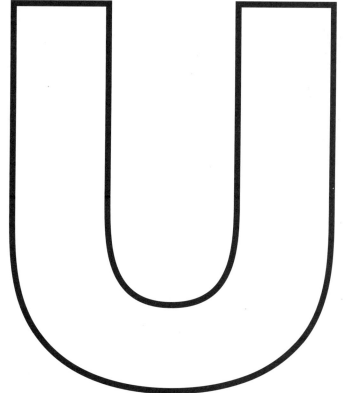

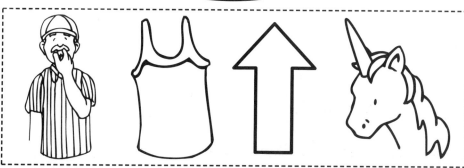

Alphabet—RBP3241

Name _____

Print the uppercase V.

Print the lowercase V.

Color Van Vulture playing the violin.

V v

Do the dot-to-dot 1–10.
Color Vicky Viscacha.
Color the uppercase letter V's gray.
Color the lowercase letter V's brown.

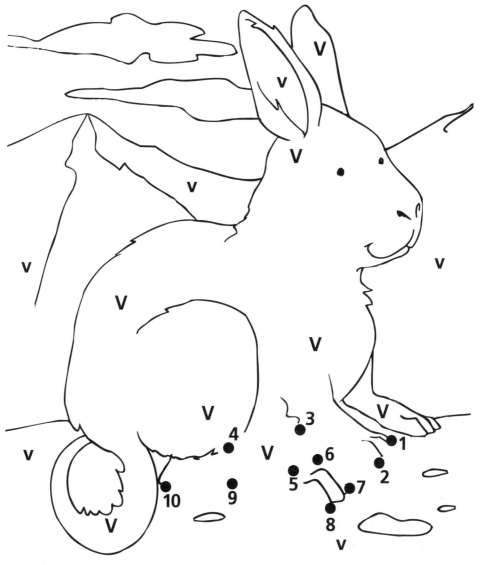

Name _____

Say each picture name.
Listen for the "v" sound.
Draw the pictures on the V, and color them.

Name _____

Ww

Print the uppercase W.

Print the lowercase W.

Color Willie Wolf whistling his warning of danger.

Name _____

Ww

Color Wayne Whale and his friends.
Color the uppercase letter **W**'s blue.
Color the lowercase letter **W**'s black.

Name _____

Say each picture name.
Listen for the "w" sound.
Draw the pictures on the W, and color them.

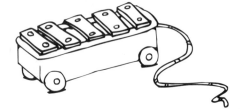

Print the uppercase X.

Print the lowercase X.

Color Rex Fox with his box and his socks.

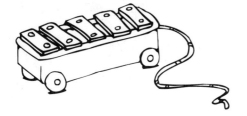

X x

Do the dot-to-dot 1–10.
Color Xavier X-ray fish.
Color the uppercase letter **X**'s green.
Color the lowercase letter **X**'s blue.

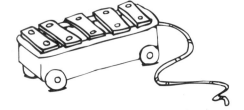

Say each picture name.
Listen for the "x" sound.
Draw the pictures on the X, and color them.

Name _____

Y y

Print the uppercase Y.

Print the lowercase y.

Color Yackety Yak playing with his yellow yo-yo.

Yy

Do the dot-to-dot 1–10.
Color Yolanda Yellowhammer.
Color the uppercase letter Y's yellow.
Color the lowercase letter y's green.

Yy

Say each picture name.
Listen for the "y" sound.
Draw the pictures on the Y, and color them.

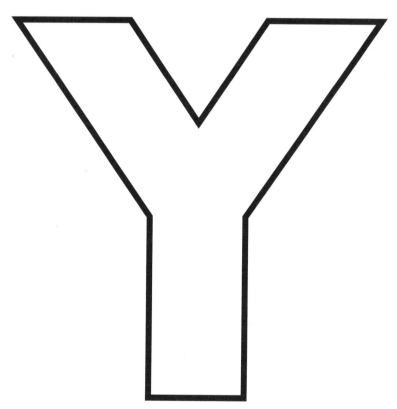

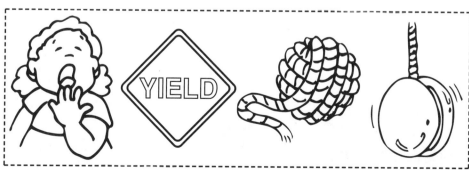

Z z

Print the uppercase Z.

Print the lowercase Z.

Color Zach Zebra eating zucchini.

Name _____

Zz

Do the dot-to-dot 1–10.
Color Zoro Zorille.
Color the uppercase letter Z's black.
Color the lowercase letter z's brown.

Alphabet—RBP3241

Z z

Say each picture name.
Listen for the "z" sound.
Draw the pictures on the Z, and color them.

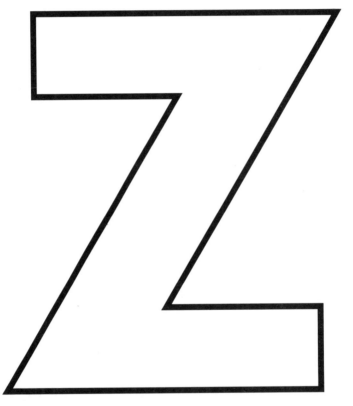

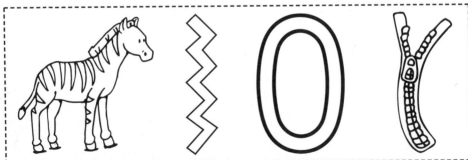